Rust + Moth
Summer 2019

Edited By: Josiah Spence, Suncerae Smith, Michael Young, and Matthew Payne.

© 2019 Rust and Moth

In This Issue —

06   **Deirdre O'Connor**
     The Hands and the Clock

08   **Michael Mercurio**
     The Bowl of the Sky

09   **Clair Dunlap**
     Spring (1922)

10   **Marie Baléo**
     Song of the Siren

12   **Suzanne Grove**
     Northern Florida, Thirteen

14   **Rachel Roupp**
     My First Stepdad was a Hunter

16   **Veronica Kornberg**
     Stream

17   **Laura Lee Washburn**
     New Moon, Bald Cypress Trail

18   **Emily Lake Hansen**
     Pharaoh's Daughter Keeps a Diary

20   **John Amen**
     Dark Souvenirs

21   **Katherine Fallon**
     Worry

22 **Alice Pettway**
   History

23 **Bojana Stojcic**
   Legal Robbery

24 **Cynthia Atkins**
   Olfactory Ballad

26 **Noor Alali**
   To The Ground

29 **Adina Kopinsky**
   Cinnamon Bark and Birth

30 **Emma Easy**
   Feather

31 **Nels Hanson**
   Revolt of the Mirrors

32 **E.A. Petricone**
   When a Friend Goes Through a Breakup

33 **Clint Margrave**
   Wood Carving Lesson

34 **Audrey Lewis**
   aflame

35 **Imran Khan**
   Don't Ask Where the White Goes

36 **Diane Callahan**
How We Are Made

38 **Caitlin Conlon**
Nesting Doll

40 **Ariana D. Den Bleyker**
America in Solitude

42 **About the Authors**

The Hands and the Clock

"One hour and 41 minutes of CPR later, a Mifflinburg toddler regained his pulse and heart rate after being submerged in icy water at least 20 minutes...the 50 people [who helped save him] include the neighbor who pulled the boy from the creek to the responding medical professional chain who kept the CPR going."
—The Sunbury Daily Item

"For about four hours, in the unrelenting sun, [Michael Brown's] body remained where he fell."
—The New York Times

Set the clock to know how long it takes

Make it March, something glittering near an edge, something stuck
in a clump of snow, maybe a bird pecking at tamped-down, faded grass

Make it August, wavery heat, McDonald's scenting the blur, exhaust,
cut grass, honeysuckle, a spill of trash

a red-cheeked day, gusts, husks, branches broken after so much
snow, almost gone now into the rush of the creek

a flush-faced, bloated day, cups, bottles, sheen of oil,
sheen of sweat, rainbows in the spray of a hose

How soon the lungs filled is a question, how soon the slowed hearts stopped,
how many breaths were allotted and by what

or whom—not God, though the idea of God hovered,
and not the clock of the sun, but the pressing

heels of many hands, *for, for, for, for,* and pumping,
a single finger, six times *against*.

The Bowl of the Sky

When my mother died she broke
the bowl of the sky; I stretched
a soft cloth across the gap,
covered my nakedness, my rage.

The limits of that gesture
were slowly revealed as all things are,
but tell that to me then.

I knew hot tears, nights spent wandering
clad in glittering pieces. I fell asleep at dawn.

From then until now I didn't recognize
what moves above my head as living:
birds, bats, stars, comets. All arrive
and depart, describing arcs.

I trace their paths
with charcoal
on butcher paper.

Clair Dunlap

Spring (1922)

—after Georgia O'Keeffe

consider that the midwest never cared whether you liked it.

consider that a salmon will never remember you setting it out
in the cold stream, that algae do not have eyes to have ever
seen your eyes gazing, you touch the water and it touches you back
but the sea is a wild thing.

consider that the northwestern corner of what we call the continental united states
feels no attachment to your body, but rather to the act of your body
decaying along its fringes, the act of your body
as soil. consider this is how it would prefer you.

consider a girl as turquoise rush
who watches the icicles with the same intent,
who waits for the lilac bushes to burst
who takes a fraction of lake into her hands
ten thousand times each summer

consider the slick leaves on your parent's street
and how they do not consider you.

and isn't it, if we're being honest with ourselves,
the way that nature clangs against us like we are
fistfuls of discordant bells
that makes us love it so

that makes us curl up in it
to name it home.

Song of the Siren

1.
In the house are three effigies, carved out and hollowed to leave room for the fire.
In the kitchen, fingers doused in olive oil dig deep into recomposed meat; lips move to the sound of Hallelujah.
Under the closed door slithers the spirit of discord, or something like it; its stain crawls across the flannel pants, licks the ribs, circles the long fingers laced around a wine glass.
Three mouths, two plates, one failure: Welcome home.

2.
The bedroom emits a scream which beckons like the *adhan* calls the faithful. I want to see.
And I see: the bed is a coffin.
On it is my mother, or a sarcophagus, or a pirogue.
On it is an open mouth, or a wound, or a tear. Its sound is a tornado, a fountain springing upward.
My father looks in silence, in reverence, at the altar, an animal sighting in the wild.
There are many possible answers, but I won't be given one, and I don't understand the question.

3.

When my mother is gone, I sneak into her closet
and put on her black dress, patent heels, brown
lipstick.
And consider: how long the leg has become,
how thin the ankle below the trim.
Everything smells like her.
When my father is gone, I search for his gun. It
won't be found, but I can hear it somewhere
inside the walls — a vibration, a song; low as a
whisper, but it wants me hard.

Suzanne Grove

Northern Florida, Thirteen

It began in a season of cicadas,
of somersaulting, of popsicle-lick,
of even the dull cramp and frank blood
unable to shake us into transformation.

We had spines that wanted
no attention.

Until the pool days, chlorinated
and showing us our apathy
for the lip line, the hip
jut, the ransom the others put on their bodies.

So we trimmed our fine fuzz
and slicked our legs with oil.

We roamed baseball fields
and pulled everything into death—
the tall grass, the lightning bug, the
Virginia Bluebells turning away in disappointment.

We played at it
before we felt it like a hot
slice down the core,
exhuming whatever sense of personhood we had.

A throb, a gnawing
oh god we thought we'd invented it.
Disappeared across the chasm
only once thinking it possible to step backwards.

As a last attempt, we ran so
the muscle separated from the fat
but we knew then we were nourishment
for ourselves and all flesh
for someone else.

My First Stepdad was a Hunter

I grew up with his woods at my back.
He only took me into them once.
I was too small and slow
for him to keep an eye on
while he was lining up his sights
with our winter meat's beating heart.

When I was five, we got a hunting dog,
a beagle he clutched against his red chest.
After looking into her full, brown eyes,
he could only shoot bucks, said
her face was just too much like a doe's.

What did he see in my mother's eyes
when I watched his fist come up,
catch her jaw?
He clattered her teeth
like antlers rattling to conjure
a fight, a shot, a killing.

When she growled *get out,*
he grabbed his gun.

Rachel Roupp

The day he left for the last time,
he sat, cradling our beagle.
She turned out too gun-shy for hunting.
He loved her anyway.
He wanted her to stay gentle.

I've never fired a gun,
never taken aim, never
gotten the taste of buckshot
off the back of my teeth.

Stream

I dipped my fingers into the trilling
rush of you
and the blond grass stood straight
in the fields of my arms.

New Moon, Bald Cypress Trail

Where leaf break and pine blue the ground,
needles and cones lift fragrance in congress with the soft acidic rot of root
    and vine.

Mourning doves croon away and away.
Nightjars fall to their black feasts.

Cypress knees eternally stretch or bend in water so black it drinks clean.

The pirates are long ago gone. Their treasure chests, if ever they were,
sink deeper toward the core of never been

in this little song of croak and lift and the old moon falling again.

Emily Lake Hansen

Pharaoh's Daughter Keeps a Diary

I am not dumb. I knew
you would leave. I watched

from my high window
that early morning

as you ran away, your feet
kicking up a parade

of dust. I remember kissing
your toes, each piggy each

bird's claw raised to my lips –
I love you. I didn't say it

enough, no one does. And
in that opening dawn

I wondered if you knew. If
you had asked, I would

have followed you to God
still in my bathrobe, the loose

ties fanning across the dirt.
I would have opened

Emily Lake Hansen

my womb up, cut out
my insides to give you

a nest, would have stood
in front of the Pharaoh's gun –

my son, what can I do
to call you back?

Dark Souvenirs

—for Richard

I studied your craft,
how you drove the demon of gluttonous age
from its hiding place,
freeing the infant who starved for 84 years,
pang & its host
dismantled w/ a single twitch.
Little mess, little clean-up,
nailbrush, toothbrush, soapy sponge.
No mention in the real-estate ad,
the previous owner's
impeccable marksmanship.
No way to preserve your opus,
air that still trembles,
trying to catch its breath.
Memory does its best
to salvage a keepsake
–pulp, bullet, bone,
a new constellation in the night sky–
but symbols are lost,
art fails, except as it screams at the dead.
I hope what remains of you
can recognize my voice.

Katherine Fallon

Worry

The way I talk to you
when you are not here
(which is always, always),

is much like the manner
in which my dog approaches
all dead things: constant,

violent worrying from which
he derives such unthinking joy.

History

In Texas, we open windows
for tornadoes; their churning breath
does more damage behind latched glass.
Dust storms are a different story.

Mama mistook the two one summer,
and our insides filled with red dirt,
the stuff of potters' studios, of cracked yards
and dead grass. No matter

how many times I rotate the earth
under me, I am still saturated with the particles
of places before, a powder so fine
my lungs resist even the effort of a cough.

Bojana Stojcic

Legal Robbery

steal me from places, from other people's glances
from cold soups and colder wars
passing sentence after sentence
in an avalanche of speech sounds with no commas
and a word order in which the object always comes before
the period and after everything else
steal me from a time continuum creased between my eyebrows
from *who in blue blazes is making all that noise at*
the rear of the audience after screaming blue murder
what if i don't want to get out of my blue funk and get back to
what was it again?! maybe it's just this dismal weather we've been
having the reason for my blues and maybe one day
i'll stop bristling when i hear how beautiful i look in blue

steal me from a frantic search for answers, adjusting schedules, reciting
shopping lists by heart, estimating how fast to run to catch a shooting
star and driving through yellow and red lights, from two-dimensional realities
with the illusion of depth, from a plurality of overlapping sequences and
durations, steal me from conformity to facts and ideals of right conduct, from
exactness, last-minute kisses, and accepted values for quantities

steal me from myself
slow me down to a speed of
no beats per second and until all i see is
the uncontrollable laughter of the waves

Olfactory Ballad

It's Chicago, November—Wind blows
through your lunchbox like a future lover.
For now, you're ten, and such things
wait in the wings, in the vivid theater
    of your imaginings. Factory smoke
hollering where the *Marlboro Man*
is on a horse in bell-bottoms
and a bulging crotch on the *Dan Ryan Expressway*.
Truckers honk diesel. You're a little girl
    going to the Cubs game—Hot dogs dripping
with mustard. Each scent archived
as the crowd waves into
a human peace sign.
    Sometimes the darkness lifts
as an odorless perfume, derivative
as the daily ache that smells rancid
as road kill. The smell of diesel
in my family tree, DNA held in cells.
    I pricked it to see blood
show up like an out-of-town relative
looking for a quilted bed in my skin.
The snow is getting dirtier on the curbs.
Salt and Sulphur, this is how God
    lights the matchstick. I pop a doll
for the pain, but a wolf still sniffs
me out in every plinth and corner.
My favorite sound is silence.

My favorite smell is sex after hugging
legs tight around the hips of a man
    that knows my flaws
and loves me any way. After my son's birth,
for months, even washed, my nightgown
held the netted smell of a pause
just before life ticks in. My son
scowled his first breath, it hit like a package
    thrown to the stoop. He was the cure hugging
the poison. In this life, I've learned to smell
by memory, all the ways we slight
each other without ever knowing it.
Flowers on the highway. Dying is lonely.

To The Ground

A nurtured weed
Where bodies become
fertilizer.
(He becomes
a black mist).
Smoke without any blood.
— $C_{10}H_{14}N_2$, Nicotine

Wrapped in white casing
They unfold into Blackness
Into him.
Merely cooked, not burned.
Yet.
— Medium Rare

"Why can't he talk or move?"
Silence.
Not a gun not a knife not a car crash
He became that black mist, smoke
(but without any blood)
— Stained

They say he had colored eyes
Green.
I remember the sounds of machines whirring.
I do not remember his eyes.
They were closed shut.
They say he had a warm voice.
Deep.
Yearned for.
Like rain in a desert.
I do not remember his voice.
I remember being afraid
to go near that blank body
It took all his breath.
— Memory

With 16 years plugged in to the hospital walls
Walls made of cement
Cement made to stay
Even before I was born
We were waiting for that cement to dissolve
— Barrier

Noor Alali

What if I could be it
He loved spending time with it
Leading him by his hands
His rough, wrinkled, worked hands
What if I could be the one in his grip
I could get broad green leaves that would be dried out and rolled up
Rolled up tight in his breathing hands at least once
— Grasp

Breathe in
Breathe out
Breathe in
Breathe out
Breath in the toxic smoke
and let it take your lungs.
— Air

I was too late
No
It wasn't me
Maybe I–
No
It wasn't me
I should have–
No
— Goodbye

Adina Kopinsky

Cinnamon Bark and Birth

When I met you, I smelled cinnamon bark and resin —
yellow like beeswax, riesling, jaundice,

the peeled underbelly of citrus. Pith and cord, seed and syrup.
Blood and wine a double helix wrapped around your neck.

Maracas of clove and straw. The sommelier says you can taste it.
The smell of embers at a barbeque, sweat; a shower can't wash off this memory.

Your body laid on my chest, streaks of white and red, vernix
fuses us like melted wax, each exhalation rises

like incense from the flame, disperses us into breath —

Feather

Upstairs, we can stand on the sill
look down at the backyards
a sorrow of outhouses
and upturned cisterns
tarpaulins flung weeping
rust crumbling up a dead bike
see a sparrow
pluck from a silk strand left under the stem
the prize of a semi-plume

white as a sclera
a perfection of keratin
it grew deep in the dark
of a gull's breast
was nourished
served devotedly with barbs
against the horror of cold
until its collar grew slack
and it fell.

Always, this preference for the new.

Dedicated to life,
it's carried with a chirrup
to a crack in the eaves
of my temple
and adding its weight
to the jumble
of paper and string
it glows fat in the dark
like a poem

Revolt of the Mirrors

All along, a few, the silent ones,
sensed the day was coming,
knew even sky and water,
the silent earth reach their
limits and say no
though the first to revolt
were the mirrors who one day
refused our reflections, returning
only faces of fathers, mothers,
their parents, backward, backward,
a rush of flashing unknown eyes
until smoke from an original fire
and pure blankness forever
like a pupil with a cataract.
Nothing in the glass, nothing,
not the wall behind you,
the peeling plaster, the green
towel on its rack, a framed
print of Van Gogh. Nothing,
nothing anymore repeating us
and ours and what we've done
as we wait for the sky and the river,
the earth to finally say no more.

When a Friend Goes Through a Breakup

I wish I could cut off your pain like hair, I tell her.

> (But all I really want to do is comb it
> —just me, over and over, until my fingertips blot with oil.
> Because the truth is this is when we are closest.)

Tell me everything, I say.

Wood Carving Lesson

Every time Mr. Stu says "wood,"
I hear *word*.

"*Wordcarving* is the process of cutting
and shaping of the *word*," he says,
with his thick Bulgarian accent.

"It is a craft with a rich history..."

He has set up a block of *word*
for our lesson today.
He takes two screws and drills them
to a base to keep the block steady.

"The type of *word* is very important," he says.
"Some *word* is softer than others. Some more
difficult to shape. But all *word* is alive."

He shows me how to hold the chisel
and how to apply pressure. I tap it with the hammer
and carve a line into the block,
like pen into paper.

Audrey Lewis

aflame

the bench had rotted,
wood growing soft and pliable
from months of too much rain,
mold and algae forming
in never-ending puddles;

so we tore it apart
and pried out the nails,
left them to rust on the patio table.

the bench, we burned.
a rain-ruined copy of
Norton's American Literature
we ripped apart for kindling
watched the letters flicker
and fade into smoke

rising above the summer night
filling our throats, our lungs
between sips of sweet cold sangria.

I could smell it in your hair for days.

Imran Khan

Don't Ask Where the White Goes

In the end, the cabinet doesn't care.
Bone-hued rounds shimmy your brain,

and who could save you from the choiring black?
Each of our Gods switched for an off-the-shelf supplement.

I watched you ride those prescriptions, like rodeo pigs,
to some unconcerned paradise.

I felt the sun stride in and out of your mouth,
heard the deals you cut with devouring,

a free admission to the back of your throat.
A trade to powder-fuck yourself helpless.

I know now I didn't know the cue and the call,
that rushing gurgle nailing your steps to the sky.

Diane Callahan

How We Are Made

On the Big Island, we learn
how the bees dance
among other songs—
the music of the ohi'a lehua blossoms
exploding in fireworks of red and yellow,
their sweetness trapped in jars of liquid gold.
This is how honey is made.

Rain draws the contours
of the world's wild places
until they sharpen into focus—
not with a polite pitter-patter
but a dizzying downpour drenching
the rocks, the earth, our very being.
This is how waterfalls are made.

The steep road to Waipi'o Valley unfolds
homes of ancient kings, and when we catch
our breath in the taro fields below—
a second-honeymoon couple, with Aloha spirit,
offers a ride back up, up, and up, and our
shaka sign, pinky and thumb, means "thank you."
This is how kindness is made.

Diane Callahan

Our bikes slice through dark lava fields
like cutting a pan of warm brownies
freshly made by the goddess Pele—
her volcanoes spit livid fire
and exhale white smoke,
shaping the sacred land into something more.
This is how the world is made.

Kapa Radio sings, "Come rub up on my belly
like guava jelly," and the frogs chirp
coqui, coqui, coqui, in our cliff house dwelling—
white plumeria perfumes my hair, a baby gecko
hops on your finger, you fall in love
while lying on picnic tables, drinking galaxies.
This is how we are made.

Nesting Doll

My grandmother's death is a big grief — the size of, maybe, a medicine ball. Anything bigger than that is no longer grief, it is hopelessness, which is generally much worse. Nobody talks about it, it being hopelessness, without lying at least a little bit. I do not want to lie, anymore. Lying is a plum sized grief. When I was younger I treated truth carelessly and I cannot tell you why, only that the guilt never tasted quite as bitter as it should have. Guilt is a watermelon sized grief. Premature forgiveness is a peach. There is something terribly fitting about eating loss when you are able to. I have not always been able to. Misplacing love for the first time was a wad of taffy as big as my head. I crawled away with a cavity on my canine but at least I crawled away. The trick is to stop believing you will come away unscathed and, instead, prepare for the inevitability of upheaval. One time my grandmother asked me if she was the reason that I was always so sad and I told her the truth, which was that I don't know why I'm always so sad. What I should've said, what she probably needed to hear, was *you are the opposite of what is misprinted in my foundation,* but I've never really been one for saying the right thing at the correct time, which, of course, is why I write, why I am here at all, meditating on grief, trying to say something that sounds nicer than *I would like you to come home, now. I would like you to take your shoes off by the coat rack and leave me notes on the kitchen counter, brag about me to your friends as I turn into a strawberry, take me to terrible matinee comedies and pretend we both hated them. I promise that, if you do, I'll stop talking to loose change on the sidewalk, poking at the birth mark on my chest that isn't there anymore, eating the flowers we once planted so carefully by the big tree. Dolly, they taste so sweet, and fresh. Like a place I could finally be happy in.*

Ariana D. Den Bleyker

America in Solitude

Today a woman rakes in the shallows,
then bends to receive the last rays of shimmering
water, her long shadow knifing the bay.
She moves to watch the sky flame
over sand flats, a hawk's wind arabesque,
an island risen, brown Atlantis at low tide;
she probes the shoreline & beyond grassy dunes
for where land might slope off into night.

Hers is no common emptiness, but a vaster silence
filled with gulls' cries, an abundant solitude.

In perfect solitude, there's fire.

She walks, the beach ablaze
with dogwood in full bloom to her side,
a bleached shirt flapping alone on a laundry line,
arms pointed down. The sun is setting.

She exhibits four clams like racehorses at auction:
Buttercup, Holland, Crimson Tide, Lucky Lady.
She picks one up & in its cold jolted memory:

a gull building strength to fly at any moment, leaping
from the sand, whirling into the air, burning
in light & raving in shadow. A lonely small gull
flying through desolation & grasslands,
lightless color, the way one understands
some true heart is feeling blue shores, clouds,
the color of every grain of sand drying
water arising as perfume,
every inner murky small grain beaten alone,
its grit, the individuality dark flume.

Wanting more she knows beauty strikes just once,
hard, never in comfort, for that better fruit,
tasting of earth & song. She'd risk exile.
She would forfeit mist for hail,
put on a robe of feathers,
& run out broken,
to weep & curse—for joy.

About the Authors

Deirdre O'Connor is the author of *The Cupped Field*, which received the Able Muse Book Award and is forthcoming soon and *Before the Blue Hour* (Cleveland State, 2002). She directs the Writing Center at Bucknell University, where she also serves as Associate Director of the Bucknell Seminar for Undergraduate Poets.

Michael Mercurio lives and writes in the Pioneer Valley of Massachusetts. His poems and reviews have appeared in *The Indianapolis Review, Crab Creek Review,* and *The Lily Poetry Review.*

Clair Dunlap grew up just outside Seattle, Washington, and started writing at the age of six. She is the author of *In the Plum Dark Belly* (2016) and her work has appeared or is forthcoming in *Love Me Love My Belly* (Porkbelly Press), *The Oakland Review, Glass: A Journal of Poetry, Hobart,* and more. She currently lives in the Midwest and answers research questions in a library.

Marie Baléo is a French writer born in 1990. Her work has been nominated for a Best of the Net, Best Microfiction and Best Small Fictions, and her work has appeared or is forthcoming in *Passages North, PRISM International, Yemassee, Litro, Tahoma Literary Review,* and elsewhere. She is an editor at *Panorama Journal.*

A graduate of the University of Pittsburgh, **Suzanne Grove** received the J. Stanton Carson Grant for Excellence in Writing while continuing her studies at Robert Morris University. She has poetry forthcoming in *The Penn Review* and has published travel essays. She is a reader for *CRAFT* literary magazine.

Rachel Roupp is a poet from the mountains of Mansfield, Pennsylvania. Her work has appeared in *Crab Fat Magazine, Chantwood Magazine, Persephone's Daughters,* and *Rag Queen Periodical,* where she serves as the Social Media Coordinator. She just wants Dolly Parton to be proud of her.

Veronica Kornberg is a poet based in Pescadero, on the Central Coast of California. Recipient of the 2018 Morton Marcus Poetry Prize, her work has appeared or is forthcoming in *Beloit Poetry Journal, Spillway, Tar River Review, Radar Poetry, Salamander, Valparaiso Poetry Review,* and *Tinderbox Poetry Journal,* among others.

Laura Lee Washburn, Director of Creative Writing at Pittsburg State University, is the author of *This Good Warm Place* (March Street) and *Watching the Contortionists* (Palanquin Chapbook Prize). Her poetry has appeared in such journals as *Cavalier Literary Couture, Carolina Quarterly, 9th Letter, The Sun, Red Rock Review,* and *Valparaiso Review.*

Emily Lake Hansen is the author of *Home and Other Duty Stations* (Kelsay Books, forthcoming 2020) and the chapbook *The Way the Body Had to Travel* (dancing girl press, 2014). Her poetry has appeared in *Atticus Review, Nightjar Review, Stirring,* and *BARNHOUSE,* among others. She currently serves as the poetry editor of Minerva Rising Press.

John Amen is the author of several collections of poetry, including *Illusion of an Overwhelm,* a finalist for the 2018 Brockman-Campbell Award, and work from which was chosen as a finalist for the Dana Award. He is a staff reviewer for *No Depression.* He founded and edits *The Pedestal Magazine.*

Katherine Fallon received her MFA from Sarah Lawrence and works in the Department of Writing & Linguistics at Georgia Southern University. Her work has appeared or is forthcoming in *Rogue Agent, 3Elements, Permafrost, Colorado Review, Meridian,* and others. Her chapbook, *The Toothmakers' Daughters,* is available through Finishing Line Press.

Alice Pettway is the author of three books of poetry: *The Time of Hunger* (2017), *Moth* (2019) and *Station Lights* (forthcoming 2021). Her work has appeared or is forthcoming in *The Colorado Review, The Miami Herald, The Progressive, The Threepenny Review,* and many others. Pettway lives and writes in Shanghai.

Bojana Stojcic teaches, bitches, writes, bites and tries to breathe in between. Her poems and flash pieces are published or forthcoming in *Anti-Heroin Chic, Down in the Dirt, Mojave Heart Review, Dodging the Rain, The Stray Branch, Tuck magazine, X-R-A-Y Lit Magazine,* and *Visual Verse.*

Cynthia Atkins is the author of *Psyche's Weathers* and *In The Event of Full Disclosure,* and the forthcoming collection *Still-Life With God.* Work has appeared in *Alaska Quarterly Review, Apogee, BOMB, Cleaver Magazine, Cultural Weekly, Diode, Florida Review, Flock Lit, Los Angeles Review, Rust+Moth,* and more.

Noor Alali is a 14 year old from Kuwait. She is a student at the American School of Kuwait.

Adina Kopinsky is an emerging poet balancing poetry, motherhood, and reflective living. Now living in Israel, she is originally from Los Angeles and has a degree in English Literature from California State University, Northridge. She has work published or forthcoming in *Carbon Culture Review, Flyway: Journal of Writing and Environment,* and *Peacock Journal,* among other publications.

Emma Easy writes poetry and nonfiction, and lives in Cornwall, UK.

Nels Hanson grew up on a small raisin and tree fruit farm in the San Joaquin Valley of California. His fiction received the San Francisco Foundation's James D. Phelan Award and Pushcart nominations in 2010, 2012, 2014 and 2016. His poems received a 2014 Pushcart nomination, Sharkpack Review's 2014 Prospero Prize, and 2015 and 2016 Best of the Net nominations.

E.A. Petricone thinks a lot of the heart. Her work has appeared in *Slice Magazine*, *The Writer's Chronicle*, and other marvelous places.

Clint Margrave is the author of *Salute the Wreckage* (2016) and *The Early Death of Men* (2012), both published by NYQ Books. His work has appeared or is forthcoming in *The Threepenny Review, New York Quarterly, The Writer's Almanac, Rattle, Cimarron Review, Verse Daily, The American Journal of Poetry,* and *Ambit* (UK), among others. He lives in Los Angeles.

Audrey Lewis is an emerging writer living in New York, NY. She writes before, after, and all around the mundane responsibilities of life – looking for beauty in unlikely places. Despite her current east coast address, her heart belongs to the Great Lakes.

Imran Khan teaches creative writing around Southern England. His work has recently appeared, or is forthcoming, in *The Rumpus, Menacing Hedge, Juked, ucity Review, The Lake, Across the Margin,* and elsewhere. Khan is a previous winner of the Thomas Hardy Award.

Diane Callahan strives to capture her insignificant sliver of the universe through writing fantasy, non-fiction, and poetry. As a developmental editor and ghostplotter, she spends her days shaping stories. Her YouTube channel, *Quotidian Writer,* provides practical tips for aspiring authors.

Caitlin Conlon is a 21 year old writer that believes in quiet bravery. A graduate of the University at Buffalo with a BA in English and Creative Writing Certificate, Caitlin has previously been published via *Thought Catalog, Bottlecap Press, Germ Magazine, Tongue Tied Mag,* and *Up The Staircase Quarterly.*

Ariana D. Den Bleyker is a Pittsburgh native currently residing in New York's Hudson Valley where she is a wife and mother of two. When she's not writing, she's spending time with her family and every once in a while sleeps. She is the author of three collections, eighteen chapbooks, three crime novellas, a novelette, and an experimental memoir.

Cover and layout by *Josiah Spence*.

All content © Rust and Moth 2019.
Rights to individual poems revert to the authors after first publication of the issue.

ISSN # 1942-5848
rustandmoth.com

Made in the USA
Coppell, TX
07 December 2019